AMAZING RACIN S

TOURING CARS

BY ASHLEY GISH

CREATIVE EDUCATION • CREATIVE PAPERBACKS

Published by Creative Education and Creative Paperbacks
P.O. Box 227, Mankato, Minnesota 56002
Creative Education and Creative Paperbacks are imprints of
The Creative Company
www.thecreativecompany.us

Design by The Design Lab
Production by Joe Kahnke
Art direction by Rita Marshall
Printed in China

Photographs by Alamy (neil cannon, Uwe Deffner, Jakob Ebrey,
Artyom Korotayev/ITAR-TASS News Agency, Paren Raval, Juergen
Tap/DTM/ITR/dpa picture alliance, Gergo Toth), Getty Images (GP
Library/Universal Images Group), iStockphoto (urfinguss), Newscom
(Peter Blakeman/actionplus, Jason Heidrich/Icon Sportswire), Shut-
terstock (Rodrigo Garrido, vdant 85)

Library of Congress Cataloging-in-Publication Data
Names: Gish, Ashley, author.
Title: Touring cars / Ashley Gish.
Series: Amazing racing cars.
Includes bibliographical references and index.
Summary: A fast-paced, high-interest introduction to touring cars,
powerful race cars known for their strong engines and use in a
variety of races. Also included is a biographical story about touring
car driver Gordon Shedden.
Identifiers:
ISBN 978-1-64026-293-5 (hardcover)
ISBN 978-1-62832-825-7 (pbk)
ISBN 978-1-64000-423-8 (eBook)
This title has been submitted for CIP processing under LCCN
2019049699.

CCSS: RI.1.1, 2, 4, 5, 6, 7; RI.2.2, 5, 6, 7, 10; RI.3.1, 5, 7, 8;
RF.1.1, 3, 4; RF.2.3, 4

First Edition HC 9 8 7 6 5 4 3 2 1
First Edition PBK 9 8 7 6 5 4 3 2 1

Table of Contents

Touring cars look like normal family cars. But they are powerful racing machines. The first touring car races were held in the United Kingdom during the 1950s.

The first British Touring Car Championship was in 1958.

Racing rules are different from country to country.

Touring cars are based on production model cars. These vehicles have **aftermarket** parts to make them go faster and run longer. Many are covered in **sponsor** stickers.

aftermarket describing parts that are bought to replace existing parts

production model everyday, mass-produced cars

sponsor a person or company that pays for a race car

Touring cars have four or five doors. The car must meet a minimum weight with the driver inside. Touring cars have good brakes to handle challenging courses.

The bodies of touring cars start out the same, but most of the parts get replaced.

Touring cars are powerful but not as fast as Formula One cars.

Many touring cars have turbocharged engines. These engines pull in air with more force than regular engines. They produce more power without wasting much fuel.

engines machines that make vehicles move by burning fuel

Touring car races follow a formula, or set of rules. This ensures that races are fair for every driver. In some races, drivers are all required to use the same kind of tires. For others, the cars might have to use the same type of fuel or have the same size engine.

Touring car races last between 3 and 24 hours.

The top finishers might be within less than a second of each other.

The British Touring Car Championship (BTCC) is a race **series** in the U.K. Winners must carry **ballast weights** during their next race. This makes winning another race more difficult. It gives other drivers a shot at winning a race.

ballast weights weights made of heavy material

series a set of races where drivers compete for a championship

Supercars are the most powerful touring cars. They speed up quickly. Supercars can reach speeds of nearly 200 miles (322 km) per hour.

The Supercars Championship is held in Australia.

Each driver wears safety gear, such as a helmet, gloves, and fire suit.

Touring cars are used for a variety of races. Sprint races are short and fast. **Endurance** races can last up to 24 hours. Sometimes, touring cars race alongside sports cars.

endurance the ability to go continuously without wearing down

Today, touring car races are held all over the world. Check out a race near you and watch these amazing cars zip around the track!

City streets are closed to regular vehicles when a race is on.

Gordon Shedden

was 20 years old when he began racing in the British Racing and Sports Car Club (BRSCC). The following year, he won the BRSCC Ford Fiesta Championship. Gordon started racing in the BTCC five years later, in 2006. He was named BTCC Rookie of the Year. He is one of just three Scottish drivers to ever win the series. Gordon took the title in 2012, 2015, and 2016.

Read More

Bodensteiner, Peter. *Supercars*. North Mankato, Minn.: Black Rabbit Books, 2017.

Bowman, Chris. *Race Cars*. Minneapolis: Bellwether Media, 2018.

Skinner, Adam. *Fast Forward: The World's Most Famous Race Tracks and Race Cars*. Minneapolis: Wide Eyed Editions, 2019.

Websites

DK Find Out: History of Cars
https://www.dkfindout.com/us/transportation/history-cars/
Learn more about how cars have developed through time.

Kiddle: Auto Racing Facts for Kids
https://kids.kiddle.co/Auto_racing
Read more about touring car races and other motorsports.

YouTube: Final Drive TV
https://youtu.be/0Xl2ABQm23w
Watch a United States Touring Car Championship race.

Note: Every effort has been made to ensure that the websites listed above are suitable for children, that they have educational value, and that they contain no inappropriate material. However, because of the nature of the Internet, it is impossible to guarantee that these sites will remain active indefinitely or that their contents will not be altered.

Index